Kailas
Shiva's Abode

# Kailas

## Shiva's Abode

HEMANT SHARMA

Translated by

Prof. Pushpesh Pant • Dr. Hari Krishna Paliwal, IAS

Publisher • **PRABHAT PRAKASHAN *PVT. LTD.***
4/19 Asaf Ali Road,
New Delhi-110002 (INDIA)
prabhatbooks@gmail.com

Edition • First, 2020
Price • Rupees Nine Hundred only
Printer • Gopsons Papers Ltd., Noida

---

**KAILAS: SHIVA'S ABODE** *by* Hemant Sharma
ISBN 978-93-89982-79-4 ₹ 900.00

Without guru,
no one can
attain the Supreme.

# BEFORE THE BEGINNING

Hemant Sharma managed to track me down at my retreat at *Haridvanam*[1]. The narrative of a journey to Kailas[2] and Mansarovar[3] – a voyage within from Kashi to Kailas – is an exploration of one's roots, the chronicle of deliverance of ancestors and self-realisation before its publication. I am indeed indebted.

This travelogue is almost an echo of my grief at personal failure. When I started my forays into the Himalaya, the pilgrimage was open. I could have undertaken it any time but I didn't do so. When the desire became overpowering, I discovered to my sorrow that China had tightened its grip. The government's conducted tours, when launched, were not meant for me.

I then went from Kathmandu and Nagarkot till the bridge beyond which lie Tibet and the Hindu pilgrimage centres of Kailas and Mansarovar. But what can remain of the sacred when the land is under communist China's occupation? How can that reverential sentiment survive? Desire to liberate the holy Kailas and Mansarovar continued to plague me in myriad forms. Indo-Tibet Friendship Associations at Kashi, Delhi, Shimla kept raising their voice stridently. I undertook drives along the Hindustan-Tibet Road, touching Shimla, Rampur, Bushair, Reckong Peo, Kalpa, Samdu; then I walked up to Namgya, the last inhabited village on the border. Reflecting deeply, I rested for a while at the inspection bungalow at Namgya.

---

1 *Haridvanam : The Valley School and Study Centre run by Krishnamurti Foundation at Bengaluru.*

2 *Kailas : The mountain named after Lord Shiva situated in the Himalayan range and one of the most sacred Hindu pilgrimage Centre.*

3 *Mansarovar : Mansarovar is a high-altitude freshwater lake with a circumference of 81 kms fed by the Kailas glaciers near Mount Kailas. It is revered deeply and considered a highly sacred place by four religions – Bon, Buddhism, Hinduism and Jainism.*

The village headman was hospitable but the old road was in disrepair while the new one hadn't been laid – the same state of affairs as the country's. Then Geshe La said with great pain, "Please, leave us as we are. Spare Kinnaur. You are a large state (till then, Uttarakhand was its part) and let the route that passes through it be used. If China comes here via the new road, where will we seek refuge? Byela Kuppe? Mundgod? Or somewhere else?"

During this brief sojourn, I learned that four or five Chinese soldiers had visited the village recently, prompting many terrified villagers to run away. Since then, I stopped demanding the opening of this alternative route. However, I didn't stop demanding that the Kailas-Mansarovar pilgrimage should be freed of any control.

There is a third route, via Nepal's Ganjutilising by helicopter, Land Cruiser or on foot. Perhaps this option wasn't there in those days and neither did I know of it.

Anyway, now I have travelled with Hemant on this route and have accomplished the journey within. I have stood in the presence of Kailas and touched it and also taken the dip in the holy waters of Mansarovar Lake, for the first time, miraculously! What a feeling! What an upsurge of glorious language! Such evocative prose can only be written in Kashi. Nowhere else. I have read its description at many other places, like in Gagan Gill's *Avak*! I have myself described the glories of Kailas-Mansarovar – covering many white sheets of paper with my scribbling, but never have I been so totally immersed, drenched after the dip!

Can this be repeated, re-experienced? Can someone tell us?

**— Prof. Krishna Nath***

The Study
Bengaluru

*Prof. Krishna Nath was the scion of an old Benaras family well known for its philanthropy. He was drawn into the socialist movement in his youth and remained a lifelong supporter of socialism despite the many schisms that repeatedly splintered the party so lovingly nourished by Dr Lohia. Soft spoken and erudite, he was an ardent trekker who undertook many exploratory journeys in Kumaon. *Garhwal* and *Himachal Pradesh,* the two Himalayan travelogues, penned by him in Hindi, are considered miniature gem-like classics. He fiercely defended the cause of Tibetan independence.

# STEPPING OUT

How can one describe that which is beyond description? Can an undecipherable riddle ever be explained? But still one must try. Shiva is infinite and the infinite can't be contained in words – Rudra in the *Vedas* and *Puranas* and Bhairav for the tribals or Bhole Shankar for the common man and our personal friend and mentor, who was perpetually high on hash. How can all these be confined in an image? That's why, where words failed, I resorted to my camera. All the photographs in this book were clicked by me during the trip unself-consciously and in a trance-like state. These pictures unravel the mystery of Kailas-Mansarovar on their own.

My journey to Kailas was a voyage within – a quest for one's roots on a broad canvas, stretching from Kashi to Kailas. What I pursued has been explored earlier too by three other denizens of Kashi. Kabir, who dwelt in my street, wrote, *"Mansarovar subhar jal, hansa keli karahinmuktahal mukta chugain, ab udi anat na jahi".* The great poet, Jaishankar Prasad wrote in *Kamayani: "Manu ne kuchh kuchh muskakar Kailas dhikhaya. Bole dekho yehan par koi nahin paraya."* Babu Shiva Prasad Gupt, in his book, *Prithvi Pradakshina*, sheds light on the divine aspects of Kailas. This is an effort to continue to follow in their footsteps.

There is little that is said and much that remains unsaid in the book. I have remained silent at places. This is not a travelogue nor is it a memoir. If I am present in this book, so are you. With Kailas and Mansarovar. What was our point of view? What did we see? And, how much of what was seen and experienced has been described? Maybe not much. To tell the truth, this journey is still continuing within. To see God, it is said, one has to die. Those living beings who do so are *siddhas* – adepts. We were not *siddhas.* Nor did we die. But, at Kailas and Mansarovar, we were in the presence of the Divine. If I succeed in making you my fellow-traveller, it is the result of accrued good *karma (punya)*. If I have failed, the loss in mine.

Let us embark on this journey together to encounter the Infinite. If you share with me some of the transcendental bliss, I shall consider myself successful.

**—Hemant Sharma**

**Shivratri 2020**

# DEBTS THAT CAN'T BE REPAID...

- I'm deeply indebted to my ancestors whose inspiration took me to Mansarovar.
- To the mortal self that didn't fail me through the arduous journey.
- To the mind that could comprehend the surreal experience.
- My father Shri Manu Sharma, who taught me how to walk with words.
- Critic and guru, Prof. Namvar Singh, the titan who, through his mighty pen and assiduous eyes, gave my writings a new direction. His phone call every Monday accelerated the writing of this book.
- Fount of knowledge, Shri Devendra Dwivedi, whose constant persuasion pushed me towards penning down a book.
- Prof. Krishna Nath, his deep connection with Tibet and his active participation in Dr. Lohia's movement for Tibet is known to all. I am deeply indebted to him for agreeing to write the Foreword.
- Dr. Pushpesh Pant, whose multifaceted knowledge, remains unparalleled. He has undertaken the Herculean task of translating this book.
- Dr. Hari Krishna Paliwal, an officer of the Indian Administrative Services, as the Chief Secretary of Arunachal Pradesh, somehow managed to find time from his busy schedule to translate the book.
- Connoisseur of art, redoubtable Rohit Suri, coordinated the pictures.
- Naveen Tewari, the 'constant critique' by my side, for the final reading of the text.
- Shivendra Singh for his undying effort to put all the strings of this translation together.
- Rakesh Dhar Tripathi, without whom this journey couldn't have been undertaken.
- B.V. Rao, for his meticulous pen that finetuned the text.
- Barun Das for his superlative inputs, drawing on his creative genius.
- Prabhat Kumar and Piyush Kumar, for putting me under pressure to speed up the writing.
- Dr. Sandip Kumar, for research and copy-editing.
- Veena, for her patience. Writing till past midnight interfered with her sleep, but this never disturbed the peace at home.
- Ishanee, who is the first and final reader of the script in both the languages and has played an indispensable role in the production of the book.
- Parth, who most enthusiastically searched and collected special stuff required for this journey in the realm of snow.

## The Resolve

# SANKALP

What is the connection between Kashi and Kailas? Why does Mahadev, the God of gods like Kailas so much? I nurtured the wish to see the garden of Eden of sages and ascetics. Born in Kashi, ever since I came of age, I used to wonder what Lord Shiva does in Kashi if he resides in Kailas. Kailas means Heaven, whereas just by dying in Kashi one goes to Heaven. This is the eternal link between Kashi and Kailas. The idea was at the root of my resolution to visit Kailas. That I had to go to Heaven but without dying. But not everyone can go there only on invitation. Nobody from our family ever went there, not even relatives. Nobody had even imagined that one could go there while living in this body. Hence this was not just another trip for me but an inward journey. A programme to move into the memories of the past. An oblation to liberate the ancestors. The joy of being in Heaven alive. This was my reason for going to Kailas.

Shiva is the only God whose continuity remains right since the time of creation. He either lives in Kailas or at the cremation ground and Kashi happens to be a great cremation ground. Shiva is the presiding deity of Kashi. The connection between the two gets established by this very thread. Both have a very basic relation – Heaven and the way for this bridge.

Wanderlust and the desire to know the land and society more had been fuelling my wish to visit Kailas. There were many curiosities. All our major rivers have their source in the region. The largest reservoir of fresh water on earth is situated there. The celestial swans are found there. I recall that how in my childhood, my grandmother used to describe Kailas as being akin to a dreamland. According to her, Shri Krishna has said in the *Gita – Meruru shikhirinamaham* – 'Among mountains, I am Kailas!'

And, Mansarovar is also a wonderful mysterious realm. It changes colour several times a day as the sun moves along the sky. Sages and ascetics along with celestial beings come for their morning dip at *Brahmamuhurat,* just before the crack of dawn. Rimpoche[1] treats Mansarovar with the same reverence as he has for Lord Buddha. Rimpoche was the Prime Minister in the Tibetan government in exile. When he used to live in Benaras, he often visited our house. He never tired of describing the out-of-this-world beauty of Mansarovar. My understanding of Buddhism as a child was shaped by him.

It is said Brahma[2] dwells in Brahmlok, Vishnu[3] in Baikunth and Shiva in Kailas. We can't visit Brahmlok or Baikunth as long as we are alive. It's only Kailas that can be visited when alive. Shiva is the beginning; so going to Kailas is revisiting one's roots. It is a journey to the source of Ganga. It is to sit in the lap of Ksheersagar – the ocean of milk. The intimate Benaras relationship of Shiva and Ganga was pulling us towards Kailas.

---

[1] *Rimpoche : The term is used for highly respected and recognised lamas of the Tibetan Buddhist sect. Samdong Rimpoche is the former Prime Minister of Tibetan government-in-exile in India and a close associate of Dalai Lama.*

[2] *Brahma : One of the triple dieties of Hinduism. He is attributed with the cosmic role of creation. He is believed to be the Creator of Vedas.*

[3] *Vishnu : One of the gods in the Trinity and the preserver of the universe.*

Friends warned that the journey would be difficult and one should think twice before embarking upon it. But I had resolved. I had to go. Thought I should prepare my will so that no one is inconvenienced in case of a mishap. Then the thought came – if this is what pleases Him, why should I bother? We took off without a second thought on the most beautiful and arduous journey in the world. On a quest to discover the essence of Shiva, on a primordial journey, eternal and infinite at the same time. Fortified with the belief that it is Kailas, that it is Meru[1] Parvat, the Axis Mundi of the universe.

In our faith, Kailas is the abode of Shiva and Parvati[2]. The Buddhists believe that this is the place where Bodhisattva[3] descended on earth. Jains think that this is where the first *teerthankar*[4], Rishabhdeva, attained *nirvana*. They call it

---

[1] *Meru : A Mountain mentioned in the Hindu Scriptures where gods and demigods dwell.*

[2] *Parvati : Shiva's second wife and consort.*

[3] *Bodhisattva : In Buddhist belief the Bodhisattva is a person who is on the path of enlightenment, before its realisation.*

[4] *Teerthankar : The great enlightened being of the Jain religious tradition.*

*ashtpada*, as according to one mythic account, Rishabhdeva had circumambulated the mountain in eight superhuman steps.

In Buddhist tradition, the extraterrestrial form of Buddha, Demchok[1], can only be encountered at Kailas. This manifestation of Buddha is also called Dharmapal[2]. The Buddhists call Kailas, Kang Rimpoche – the treasure of spiritual riches. According to Tibetan legend and lore, Lord Buddha was conceived by Queen Maya in the vicinity of Mansarovar.

Bon pao[3] was the religion that Tibetans prophesied before the advent of Buddhism. According to Bon belief, Kailas is a nine-storeyed *Swastik*[4] peak that was used as a passage by their preceptors to descend on Earth. Waves of celestial and spiritual force engulf this peak. Whatever be their belief, the force is palpable during the *parikrama,* circumambulation, of Kailas.

It was Sage Mandhata who first set foot on this sacred soil. *Adi Shankaracharya*[5] shed his mortal body here. Guru Nanak[6] meditated here and Swaminarayana, the founder of the sect that bears his name, saw the vision of God here. He, we are told, had reached here straight from village Chapiya in Gonda district of Uttar Pradesh.

---

1 *Demchok Buddha : The Tibetan Buddhists believe that Mount Kailas is the abode of Demchok Buddha who symbolises supreme bliss.*

2 *Dharmapal : The second king of the Pal dynasty (AD 752-794) ruled over entire North India. A great Patron of the Buddhist religion, he was founder of the famous Vikramshila University.*

3 *Bon Pao : Was the indigenous religion of Tibetan people before the advent of Buddha, Characterised by animism and Shamanism.*

4 *Swastika : The symbol of great spiritual significance in Hindu religion.*

5 *Adi Shankaracharya : AD 788-820, philosopher and theologian and great revivalist of Hindu religion and most renowned exponent of Sanatana Dharma (eternal values the Hindu religion stands for), from whose doctrines the main currents of modern Indian thought are derived. He established four shrines in four corners of India for the propagation of religion. The nominated heads of these shrines till date are called Shankaracharya.*

6 *Guru Nanak : The first spiritual teacher and religious leader of the Sikh faith. Writer of the Guru Granth Sahib, he professed the slogan of 'Ik Onkar' which means 'God is one'.*

The *Ramayana* and the *Mahabharata* mention Kailas. This is where Ravana[1] had worshipped Lord Shiva. He wanted to take Kailas with him. Shiva guilefully dissuaded him from doing so. Arjuna performed penance here and received the *Pashupatastra* from Shiva. Yudhishthir proceeded heavenwards via this route. One by one, all the family members fell by the roadside; only the faithful dog kept company. Bhasmasur, the *Rakshas*, a devotee of Shiva was reduced to cinders here. Shiva had granted him the boon that his mere touch could burn anything to ashes. The moment he received the boon, he targeted Shiva. Shiva had to run to save himself. But that is another story. This is where Mansarovar was conceived and brought into existence through the powers of his mind by Brahma.

Bereaved at the death of his wife Sati, Shiva roamed around furiously enraged, striking terror everywhere. He appeared violently insane. Gods feared that in this state, he may unleash catastrophic destruction. There was no hope that Shiva's fury would subside as long as he carried the corpse. Brahma sent Vishnu to ensure that the remains of Sati were separated from him. Parts of the dead body were severed one by one. Sati's hand fell here to create the lake. That's why this place is reckoned as a *Shaktipeeth*[2]. Kailas has never been climbed. It remains untouched by mountaineers.

---

[1] *Ravana : The demon king of Lanka who kidnapped Lord Rama's wife Sita and caused the great battle in which he was killed by Rama.*

[2] *Shaktipeeth : The sacred place of pilgrimage for Hindus signifying the spots where parts of the body of Sati fell, creating a highly potent energy field.*

It is only circumambulated. This mountain is sacred. How can one step on it? One fears that Shiva may be enraged if it is desecrated. He is the destroyer. Without him, the entire world would soon be in the throes of anarchy. Other gods die. It is only Shiva who is immortal. He is easily pleased with a jugful of water and a few leaves from the *Bilva* tree. Even staunch atheists feel humbled in the vicinity of Kailas.

Today the dark shadow of civilisation has begun to fall even on Mansarovar. This lake is shrinking. The sacred water body, that once stretched across 410 square kilometres, is now shrunk to only 10 square kilometres. Consider this the rage of Nature. Had Kalidasa[1] been alive, he would have been deeply saddened to see his beloved Himalaya in this state. Is it the same Himalaya that is described in *Raghuvansham*[2] *and Kumar Sambhavam*[3]*?* Civilisation has reached a point where the divine dimensions of Himalaya are disturbed.

---

[1] *Kalidas : 4th century AD : One of the greatest poets and playwrights of all times; author of great works like Meghdootam and Abhigyan Shakuntalam in Sanskrit language.*

[2] *Raghu + vansh : Raghu—the king of the Ikshvaku lineage to rule over Ayodhya and one of the greatest in the line of kings to follow him. Vansh means the family tree.*

[3] *Kumar Sambhavam : A great Sanskrit epic written on the love life of Lord Shiva and his consort, Parvati. It contains the description of their marriage and the birth of their first child Kartikeya. It was written in Sanskrit by the legendary poet Kalidasa.*

# The Cosmic Sound ANAHAD

One question kept flashing in my mind throughout the Kailas pilgrimage – what is it in Shiva that compels people to worship him from Kailas in the north to Rameshwaram[1] in the south? Which is the magnet that unites aristocratic patricians to the destitute, the beggar and lumpen in the fraternity of his devotees – all of them treating him as their own? He is God of the proletariat. How is his realm so vast?

Rama's personality is 'restrained', hence limited. Krishna is 'liberated' but only Shiva is infinite. He is the beginning and he is the end. Maybe this is why he is the Lord of gods. Only Shiva is Mahadev[2], the great God. He is fond of festivities. He has the gift to be joyous even in death and grief, in deprivation and dejection. He trusts the faithful, who can sing and dance. This is the Shaiva tradition. German philosopher Frederich Neitze has said, "Sick societies have sad traditions." Shiva dances in cremation grounds. He is the only God to celebrate where the dead bodies are consigned to flames. Channu Lal Mishra sings: *'Khele masane mein hori digambar, khele masane mein hori! Bhoot pishach batori digambar, khele masane mein hori!'* This is the music of the common folk.

The realm of Shiva extends to foreign lands. In the 1960s, the hippies came from America to India. Their roots can be traced to the counter-culture of Greece. But Shiva, the favourite God of the hippies, was present here forever. You could even say Shiva is the original hippie. Half-naked, perpetually on a high, innocent like a child and generous to a fault, a beggar singing and dancing unabashedly – that is Shiva, the God! God of the common man, a symbol of the hungry and the ill shod, striving to free himself from social fetters. He makes one's own path, searching for new meanings to life.

---

1 *Rameshwaram : One of the most sacred Hindu pilgrimage centres where Lord Rama is said to have invoked Lord Shiva before embarking upon a march to conquer Sri Lanka. One of the biggest temples of Shiva is found here.*

2 *Mahadev : Synonym for Shiva literally means Lord of lords; one of his many names.*

This happy-go-lucky hippie lifestyle was the greatest obstacle in his marriage. Devi's[1] parents were reluctant to marry their daughter to this Bohemian. How could any parent give away his/her child to a hungry, naked, frenzied person? He had in his marriage party all the wrong kinds of guests – naked, shrieking and shouting – insane, spectral and stoned. As the procession approached, the bride's house, people started to scatter to escape disaster. The marriage procession of Shiva has ever since been a metaphor for mayhem.

In our tradition, there is no other greater God who can reconcile the opposite poles, who can harmonise contradictions in the most adverse circumstances. He can be *Ardhnarishwar*[2] and conquer Kama. He can be a householder and yet remain utterly detached. He is Neelkantha[3] as after swallowing deadly poison, he remains unaffected. When aggressive, he breaks into *tandava;* else remains gentle and benevolent. Easily enraged but at the same time, an ocean of compassion – this too is Shiva. Venomous snake and cool crescent-shaped moon adorn him alike. He has the nectar of moon and poison from the depths of the ocean. He owns *riddhi* and *siddhi* but remains aloof from both. Snake and the peacock, lion and the deer,

---

1 *Devi : Hindu goddess; embodiment of power. The all powerful form of God. Has several forms. Durga Saptashati is their most prominent scripture.*

2 *Ardhanarishwar : 'Lord who is half woman' Composite male-female figure of the Hindu God Shiva together with his consort Parvati. This symbol claims to have a clear scientific basis.*

3 *Neelkantha : Another name given to Lord Shiva after he drank poison which came out of the churning of the sea and held it in his throat.*

the bullock, all of them forget congenital enmities and sit around him in peace as equals. He fosters a socialistic creed. He, the auspicious one, is not only the destroyer but also responsible for our welfare. In other words, Shiva is the unique synthesiser and coordinator.

Shiva is truly non-aligned. *Suras* and *asuras*[1] – gods and demons – trust him equally. Rama and Ravana, both worship him. Warring armies worship him before a battle. He blesses both alike. This is why he is worshipped in north and south with equal reverence. He happily consumes poison that none else can endure for public weal. When he plays the *damaru,* the Universe dissolves into nothingness. But it is from the drumbeats of this very *damaru* that aphorisms of Sanskrit grammar emerge. Other languages in the world too have originated from these 14 Maheshwar[2] *sutras*.

Environment has become a global concern nowadays. Shiva is the first environmentalist – nature lover. He is *pashupati*[3]. Shepherd of helpless creatures. The Aryas were cutting forests to claim land for agriculture; milching cows, but devouring calves. It was then Shiva chose Nandi, the bull, as his mount to offer the aged animal his protection. He offered refuge to snakes displaced by deforestation.

No one befriends the wretched and the uncured. Mahadeva embraces them. No one lingers in the cremation ground. Shiva has made it his dwelling. It is hard to stay long at Kailas. The air is thin and plants are scarce. He set up his hearth here. Other gods use myriad substances for skin and body care but Shiva makes do with mere ash. He doesn't care a fig for what others may think. Other gods spend a fortune on their costumes. Shiva

---

1 *Sura/Dev and Asura/Daitya : Gods and demons or righteous and unrighteous, respectively.*

2 *Maheshwar : Root Mahesh (another name of Lord Shiva) Sutra – The fourteen verses attributed to Lord Shiva and which organise the 14 Sanskrit phonemes.*

3 *Pashupati : Another name of Shiva, the Lord of all living beings.*

just drapes a tiger skin round his waist. He sets out for his marriage in his usual attire. He has form and at the same time he is formless. Dr. Lohia has a very different take on him. He said Shiva was a peerless engineering genius who set the course for River Ganga.

Shiva is just. Those who transgress laws are punished. (Kamadeva)/Cupid crossed the limit and was burnt down. If anyone commits any extreme, there is the third eye to discipline him. Tibetans point out to a third eye that is discernible on Mount Kailas. The third eye is not just a myth. Modern science too has discovered a pineal gland in the brain situated behind the spot where the eyebrows meet. It is not always active but it has great sensitivity. This is the third eye of Shiva. If it opens, the Universe would dissolve. But the Universe is also sustained by the power it has.

Shiva's personality is immense. He is *Mahakal*—larger than time and death. He is omnipresent and all-encompassing. He is the troubleshooter for not only his devotees but also for other gods. He is always on the side of justice. His decisions are for the welfare of the people. It is essential to comprehend the various forms of Shiva to unravel the mysteries of life because he is always accessible to the person who has nothing else to offer but a mug of water. Perhaps this is the reason that his realm stretches from Kailas in the north to Rameshwaram in the south.

Shiva as Nataraj[1] for many may well have been

---

[1] *Nataraj : The dancing Lord Shiva.*

conceived in the south but the grand dance was first performed on Mount Kailas. The devout believe that the dance of Shiva is the expression of the cosmic law. Shiva danced every evening to sustain creation. All other gods and demigods – *kinnars* and *yakshas* – were in attendance. Worshipping Shiva meant worshipping all else at the same time. This is described in *Natrajsahastranam* and *Pradoshstotram*[1]. When Shiva seated his consort Shailputri[2], the daughter of the mountains and expressed a desire to dance, all other gods gathered. Vagdevi[3] came with her *veena* and Indra[4] with his flute, *Venu.* Brahma kept time with his claps. Vishnu displayed his virtuosity by playing the *mridangam*[5]. As Shiva sounded the *damaru* drumbeats, flowers were showered from the heavens.

1 *Pradoshstotram : 'Pradosh' is the specific period in the evening of the thirteenth day of the Hindu calendar. Pradosh Stotra or Mantra is chanted in invocation to Lord Shiva.*

2 *Shailputri : Another name of Parvati—the second wife of Lord Shiva.*

3 *Vagdevi : The Goddess of wisdom in Hindu religion.*

4 *Indra : The principal deity or the Rain God in Hindu faith. He is considered the king of gods and hence referred to as 'Devendra'.*

5 *Mridang : One of the oldest percussion instruments of India.*

## On The Move

# ANAVARAT

So, it was decided that we have to go to Shiva. Then why bother about packing – what to take and what to leave behind? One felt like leaving everything behind. But preparations at home were on a war-footing. Jackets and pants that could protect in subzero temperature were bought for me. A flashlight that could be worn on the head. Power bank to charge mobile without electricity. Raincoat to endure snow blizzards. Waterproof shoes, cap, socks, goggles and God knows what else! Medicines to combat high-altitude sickness, pocketable chemical pouches to keep warm. My wife and children saw us off at Lucknow, as if ours was the first expedition to follow on the footsteps of Tenzing Norgay and Edmund Hillary[1]. Medicines for high-altitude sickness – blood thinners like Dimox. The doctors felt if a tablet was taken in the morning, there should be no problem.

Some other friends joined from Lucknow. We reached Nepalganj via Bahraich. Nepalganj is an area of Nepal, controlled then by the Maoists. That day the Maoist insurgents had imposed a blockade. All roads were closed. We had a friend with good contacts. He enjoyed police protection. People told us that police was like a red rag to the Maoists. It was a happy coincidence that an old friend, who was once a local journalist, was the area commander of Maoist forces. He met me by chance. He extended warm hospitality to all of us and escorted us safely to the hotel.

I am not an extremist but I can't explain why this extreme act was undertaken. The official Kailas-Mansarovar trip takes 26 days. Some tours are conducted through Nepal on Land Cruisers in 15 days. But we had girded ourselves to do the circuit

[1] *Edmund Hillary, Sir: The mountaineer from New Zealand, who, along with his associate, Tenzing Norgay, scaled the Mount Everest for the first time in 1953.*

in five days. We sought assistance from a travel agency in Nepal and chartered a seven-seater helicopter. The chopper would take us to Hilsa[1] in Tibet and bring us back from there to Nepalganj. The three-hour-long journey beyond Hilsa was planned on Land Cruisers. All other stuff required for the trip – tents, food rations, and a cook-cum-guide – were to meet us at Takalakot[2]. That team had already started from Kathmandu.

Early next morning, we were at the Nepalganj airport. A seven-seater Bell helicopter was awaiting us. Weather was bad. So, the helicopter took off late for Simikot[3]. Simikot is a small village at an altitude of 10,000 feet on the Nepal-Tibet border.

Capt. Pradhan, the chopper pilot, was an experienced flyer and a genial person. But the cause of my worry was something else. He was the only pilot. Co-pilot's seat was occupied by one of our fellow passengers. The chopper took off without a co-pilot. After crossing several ridges of tree-clad mountains, we were flying over Simikot in two hours.

There was a small fair-weather makeshift landing strip at Simikot. Only 12-seater planes touched down here. These small aeroplanes were the only means of contact with the outside world for the hundred families that resided in this village. Otherwise, markets on either the Nepalese or Chinese side could be reached in seven days on foot. Rations are brought either by air or on mules. Mules take a week from Takalakot to traverse the perilous path to reach this remote village.

---

[1] *Hilsa : A village situated on the northwest frontier of Nepal. In the journey to Mansarovar, one has to enter Tibet through the village Hilsa. The river, Karnali has to be crossed on foot when one embarks upon the journey.*

[2] *Takalakot : A town in Tibet, the last town on way to Kailas mountain.*

[3] *Simikot : It is in the Humla city of northwest Nepal and an important stopover on way to Kailas Mansarovar having an airport at the height of 9,500 ft. above sea level.*

Simikot is in Nepal just for the sake of it; the presence of China is felt more palpably. It is situated in Nepal but remains cut-off from Nepalese culture. We were housed in a log-hut guesthouse near the aerodrome. What to do now? Responding to my question, Capt. Pradhan, said, "We will start tomorrow morning. Kindly rest here tonight."

"Why should we waste time till tomorrow? Why not continue onwards?" we asked.

Pradhan responded, "First you must acclimatise to this height; then we shall proceed."

"We have no problems. We are feeling fine. We can go ahead."

Pradhan laughed, "There can be distress soon." Having said this, he walked away to take rest.

Just then, all of us started feeling a strange heaviness in the head. Breathing required some effort now. One felt that the lungs remained 'thirsty' despite frequent gasping inhalations. The captain was sent for. He administered some medicines and advised us to take deep breaths, reassuring us that we would be fine by the evening. We expressed our gratitude to him. The purpose of the night halt was now clear. By night we had acclimatised well.

Next morning, we took off from Simikot to Hilsa. Hilsa is at 14,000 feet, so the chopper could not fly at full throttle while carrying a heavy load. We were transported in batches – three and four at a time.

Hilsa is a temporary settlement of 50 households. Temporary, because when it snows in winter, everyone migrates to Simikot. Karnali – a thin but roaring stream –

Tara Air

WFP

marks the border between Nepal and Tibet at Hilsa. China is on the other side of the river. A bridge that resembled the Laxman Jhula[1], spans the river and has to be crossed on foot. The Karnali river originates at Mansarovar. When it reaches India, after crossing the entire breadth of Nepal, it becomes Sarayu. After Ayodhya, it is Ghaghara. By the time it joins the Ganga near Balia, it has changed its name thrice.

We were in Hilsa. Everyone was drunk in Hilsa. They had attained supreme Buddhahood. All the households here run tea-and-snacks shops or sell wool. They depend on tourists for their livelihood. Tea and food are prepared on firewood for pilgrims arriving by chopper and this is how they eke out a living. Women manage shops and the men, high on alcohol, are above all bereft of any fascination for the Nepal-Tibet borderland. We are constrained to have tea and snacks here as we await our companions. We walk across the bridge to Takalakot when everyone arrives.

The township of Takalakot is at some distance from here but the border check-post where customs and other clearances are done is quite close. Our passports and permits are scrutinised. Our watches are set two-and-a-half hours ahead of IST. It is also checked if any of us is carrying Indian currency. You can't take Indian currency into China or take photographs of the border area.

Our first encounter with the Chinese policemen is not a pleasant one. One of the cops asks about the books I am carrying – "No picture of Dalai Lama[2] I hope?" I reply, "Not

---

[1] *Laxman Jhula : A suspension bridge over River Ganges in the city of Rishikesh in India.*

[2] *Dalai Lama : The title given to the highest spiritual authority of Tibetan Buddhism. There is a lineage of Dalai Lamas and the present Dalai Lama – Tensin Gyatso, is the 14th in the line.*

in the books but in my heart." Peeved, he stares at me. Images of the Dalai Lama are banned in Tibet. If you display such pictures in public, you can be imprisoned for 10 years.

Now we were in Tibet ruled by China. Our drivers were Tibetans. As they sighted us, they shouted, *"Bum Bhole! Har, Har Mahadev!"* This was all the Hindi they knew. The moment we set foot in Tibet, we felt, 'this is just like our Sarnath[1]!' The local people greeted us with great warmth. Language failed totally. Neither Hindi nor English was of any use. Only eyes and signs could communicate. The kids, young and old villagers, in the marketplace shouted slogans, *"Om namah Shivaya!"* Takalakot is a strategically sensitive border town in China. We could see military posts at a short distance. Arrangements for our stay

[1] *Sarnath : A Buddhist pilgrimage centre near the town of Benaras where the Buddha gave his first sermon.*

here had been made at the government guesthouse. The population is about five to six thousand. Tibetans, Nepalese and Indians, all have their markets here. There was a time when Indian traders enjoyed predominance here. Their trading was restricted with the war in 1962. Even then there are some 30-40 Indian shops; the rest belong to Tibetans and Nepalese.

Takalakot customs checked our passports and permits once again. Only after this were we allowed to proceed. At this junction we met our cook and guide from Kathmandu, along with the truck full of supplies. The truck housed a complete kitchen, replete with cooking utensils, drinking water, oxygen cylinders, medicines for everyone and a special jacket. The dinner was prepared by these people. The Nepalese guide was busy telling us that we shouldn't go to a Chinese shop for eating, lest they were to feed us dog or cat meat, maybe monkey! Tibetan driver, Gumpha Dorzi couldn't hide his resentment against the Chinese. He was curious to know about the Dalai Lama and the Tibetan refugees in India. We let him know of our affection and sympathy for the Tibetan refugees. Our relationship was now at a level of intimate friendship.

Things were the same here. *'Surya ast pahari mast!'* As the sun goes down, the hill folk get high! The town was filthy. We had nothing else to drink but tea. But beware, Tibetan tea is salted. And to make matters worse, it is topped with yak butter. I had tea only once during the entire trip and that too to express solidarity with the Tibetan friends. I had to pinch my nose and gulp it down to do this.

The pilgrims on a tour conducted by the Government of India – come via Dharchula in Uttarakhand and reach Takalakot first. This way Takalakot is closest to the Indian border. You may call it the gateway to Mansarovar.

## Wonder of Wonders

# ACHAMBHA

We were to spend the night in the guesthouse at Takalakot. The distance to Mansarovar by car took just about an hour-and-half. Therefore, we decided to spend the night in a camp on the banks of the lake. This is because I had read in books that the celestials come to bathe there at dawn. An amazing play is enacted – mighty constellations of power streak the sky. This curiosity was what fuelled this desire. We set out for Mansarovar in our respective vehicles before dusk.

We were driving on a plain between the hills. At a distance were hillock-like mountains and hillocks. Broad roads without potholes; winding up and down. This caused other vehicles to disappear at times. Such a vast desert-like plain at such a height was awe-striking. Fine-grained soil. Neither a pass nor a valley in sight. No terrifying heights, though serpentine rivers followed us all along. Mountains on one side, turquoise stream on the other. This was the highway to heaven.

On the left, Nanda Devi[1], Dhaulagiri[2] and Trishul[3] could be seen. Beyond lay India. After driving for two hours, the driver said, "Look to the left, sir!" What was this? The dream come true! Bang in front stood Kailas, shining white and radiant. The driver stopped the car. All of us got down. We kept clicking photographs. No one was prepared to move. The driver tugged, "Let's move on! The sight will be much better."

On the other side, below road level, lay Rakshas[4] Tal. You can't offer worship or perform any rites at this lake at an altitude of 15,000 feet. Tibetans believe that only evil spirits dwell there. The guide informed us that it was at this site that Ravana had performed austerities to please Shiva and asked for the boon to transport him to Lanka along with Kailas. Gods were worried that now they would have to travel to Lanka to worship Shiva. They hatched a conspiracy. When Ravana was looking away, he handed over Kailas to Ganesha[5], requesting him not to place it on the

[1] *Nandadevi : The second highest peak in the world. Mountain in the Himalaya range.*

[2] *Dhaulagiri : The Himalayan range of mountains in the north-central part of Nepal and at 8,167 metres it's the seventh highest peak in the world.*

[3] *Trishul : Trident, a weapon carried by Lord Shiva.*

[4] *Rakshas : Monster or demon.*

[5] *Ganesha : Son of Lord Shiva and Parvati, elephant-headed deity, God of wisdom and learning, bestower of well-being and remover of obstructions.*

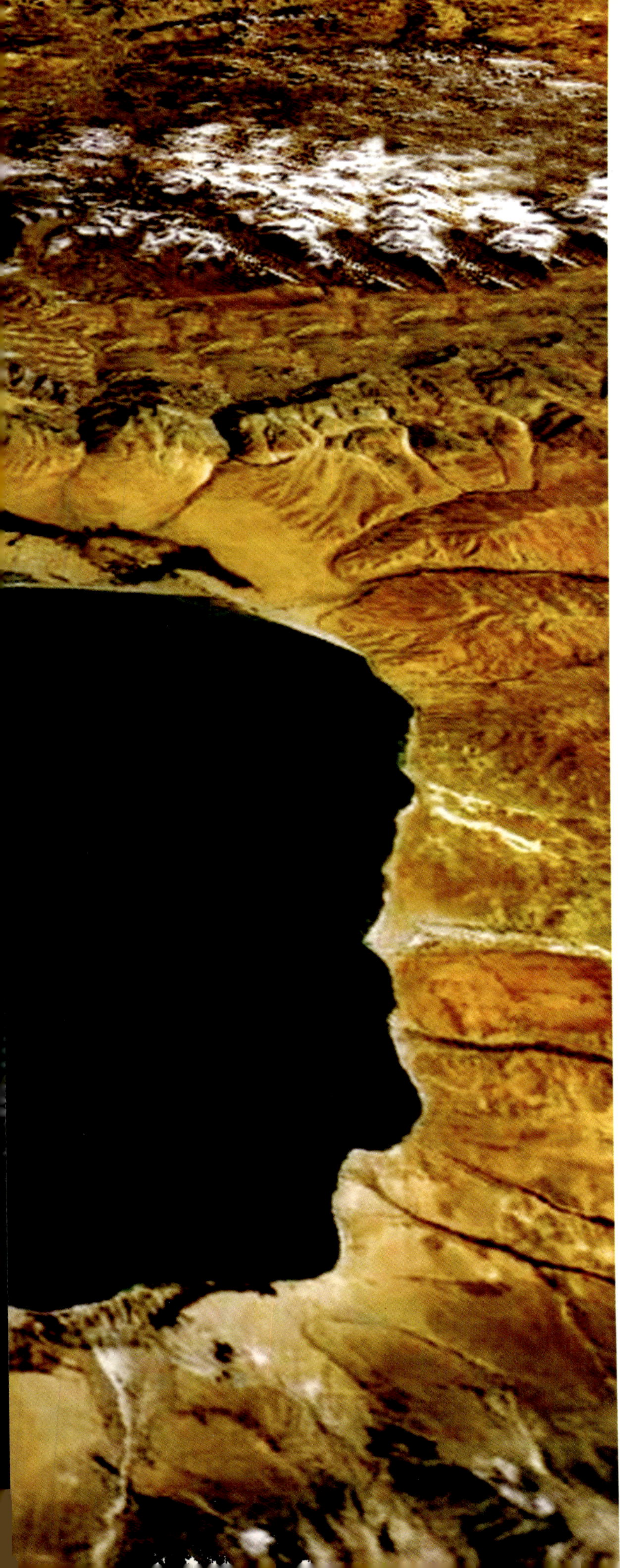

ground till his return. Ravana took hours to relieve himself and Ganesha placed the mountain on the ground. Ever since, it has remained steadfast.

The boon granted to Ravana could be used only once. Kailas was saved from exile to Lanka. This lake, according to local tradition, was created by Ravana. It is not sacred, but profane. There are many legends associated with Rakshas Tal, spreading over 250 square kilometres. Ganga Chu, a small river, connects the two lakes. The waters of this lake are dark. Black colour represents poison. This seems to be divine play. Mansarovar is nectar and Rakshas Tal is poison. Kailas is the abode of Shiva and Shiva holds poison in his body to save humanity. Scientists too believe the water in Rakshas Tal to be toxic because it has a very high mineral content. It was 8 o'clock in the night, but both Mansarovar and Rakshas Tal were shining. It was daylight till 9 p.m. at Mansarovar. Time was passing. Man-made civilisation was leaving us. Before us stood Mount Gurla Mandhata. It was King Mandhata who discovered Mansarovar and first worshipped on its banks. That's why this mountain bears his name.

This was it! Mansarovar! Suddenly we were at Mansarovar! Wonderful! Out of this world! Spell-binding! We lost our senses. Unparalleled – a land of fantasy – an infinite water body flanked by mountains. Far away near the horizon the lake seemed to be merging into the sky. I kept looking at it as if in a trance for hours. The Nepalese guide warned us, "Please put on your jacket. It is very cold." I was lost in the play of rising and subsiding waves. Beautiful fish approaching the bank with the waves added to the spell. Fishing at Mansarovar is banned but receding waves left behind a few. People collect them. They are considered a lucky charm and believed to protect man from the biting cold.

The wind was biting. We were chilled to the bones. We were given special jackets for protection as the temperature was well below zero. I was wearing clothes weighing more than 20 kg. Even then, the cold couldn't be contained. This side of Mansarovar is called Zaidi camp. One room caravan *serai*-type accommodation is constructed here. Chidanand Muniji from Rishikesh also has his *ashrama* here. He is the only Indian who has been permitted to build his *ashrama* here. There were a few shops with dried yak meat hanging on the rooftops. Locals suck on its pieces as toffees. Yak meat is heat-generating and helps one get rid of the cold.

There were three beds in each room. As soon as we entered our rooms, trouble started. Migraine hit someone, vertigo and breathing trouble bothered others. With a headache, my capacity to think clearly was affected. I hit the bed, covering myself with six or seven blankets without removing the jacket, cap, muffler, gloves and the socks. The *sherpa* guide came to my rescue with an oxygen cylinder. He rubbed a thick oil of some Tibetan medicinal plants on my temple and feet. The application of this oil worked like magic. Consciousness returned.

Cooking had started in the next room. The cook accompanying us made us drink hot Tibetan soup. Some friends were still breathless. They snuggled in the bed with oxygen cylinders. The cold outside was terrifying. No one had the strength to go out to eat. The guide told us that he would bring our food to us, warning that our troubles could aggravate if we skipped the meal. We settled for eating only *khichdi.* The guide directed us not to venture out in the night or visit the toilet alone without a stick in our hands. The dogs here are ferocious, he warned.

But we had to unravel the mystery of Mansarovar at dawn. This was the curiosity that made sleep impossible. I kept waiting for daybreak. Woke up at about three thirty, picked up my camera and stepped out of the room. Sacred Mansarovar stretched out in front. I approached the lake all alone. Fifty steps and I was standing at the bank. Blue transparent water! Holiest water of our civilisation. I sprinkled some on my head and took a ritual sip (*achaman*). Bowed to Mount Kailas glistening ahead. Stood spell-bound. There was a music in this silence. Sublimity of this musical sound of silence is

described in the *Ramayana* and the *Mahabharata, Skandapurana*[1]. Banabhatta's[2] *Kadambari*[3], Kalidasa's *Kumarsambhava* too have moving descriptions of the 'out of this world' beauty of the place.

The stars in the sky were so bright that even without moonlight, Mansarovar sparkled like silver in their glow. The lake was changing colour every moment from different angles. Excited, I kept switching between the camera's view-finder and the naked eye to capture the ethereal beauty of Mansarovar. I had heard from my grandmother that nymphs and demigods and sages came here at night. I kept waiting for their arrival in hushed silence. Lost in myself, I didn't realise when the lake had turned golden. Wonderstruck, I was transported to a different plane.

Just then, I saw a cluster of bright light. One could hear lots of people in the distance, but no one could

---

1 *Skandapurana : One of the eighteen Puranas or scriptural books of the Hindu religion.*

2 *Banabhatta : The greatest prose writer in Sanskrit language; author of famous 'Kadambari' and 'Harshcharit' was a courtier of King Harshvardhan of Kannauj.*

3 *Kadambari :The first novel written in Sanskrit language by Banabhatta in the 7th century.*

be seen. I stood still, stunned. The temperature below zero, piercing wind and freezing cold. But who cared about the cold? I was feeling as if I had found untold riches. Kept standing by the side of the lake, wondering what I should do. How could I gather and store this bliss forever? I was not able to understand anything. I was like a pauper who suddenly finds that he has been gifted infinite riches. It was as if some festival was being celebrated there.

What I saw, what I experienced is difficult to describe; it is beyond words. Bliss is silence. Speechlessness is bliss. Just then I noticed a constellation of bright light. At a distance, I could hear some people. I stood stunned, speechless. It is impossible to describe what I saw and felt – absolutely beyond words.

By now, the sun had risen. Sunlight made the water in the lake appear thicker. I turned back and was petrified. A pack of dogs blocked the way. I was terrified. I had read a lot of literature on Mansarovar before embarking on this journey. According to some accounts, the dogs here are carnivorous. They are prone to attack silently, stealthily, but these dogs were standing in a stoical posture.

For the first time, I realised that knowledge makes us cowards. Terror has no power over ignorance. I knew that the Tibetans don't cremate their dead. The corpses are cut up by the Lamas and the pieces are strewn out in the open to be devoured by vultures and other birds. Birds are hard to

come by at such heights, so it's the dogs who normally eat them. They acquire a taste for human flesh. I was getting even more nervous as I recalled all this.

Sliding slowly while engrossed in these thoughts, I had somehow managed to retreat about 30 steps. Now about 20 steps remained. I turned my back and broke into a sprint-like Usain Bolt. I saw the guide with an amused look on his face. He said, "Hadn't I warned you not to venture out alone?" Only when I had reached the safety of my room that I could breathe a sigh of relief. I was breathless but with a sense of great relief.

I had just about recovered from this misadventure when another challenge emerged. There were no arrangements in this camp for morning ablutions. Everything had to be gotten rid of in open air. To relieve ourself outdoors was no less than engaging in a battle. Roofless Indian style lavatories had been constructed here. There was no curtain or screen to ensure privacy. We Indians are quite used to standing in a line but I couldn't reconcile to the idea of queuing up for this job. I thought it much better to dispose of my digested waste in an open ground. To maintain precarious balance on two stones while clad in jacket, cap, muffler, gloves and boots was an exercise worthy of a gymnastic circus.

Icy winds pierced like sharp pins. Clothes were an unbearable burden. Stormy gusts and above all, the terror of dogs. But what else was the option? The objective was grand. I can't describe how I managed to accomplish this mission. All I can share is that I returned to the camp, strutting like a world champion. It seemed I was doing the laps at the Lord's ground with the tricolour in my hand fluttering in the wind and people applauding my victory.

*Poori* and *sabji* at Mansarovar! Great Benarasi breakfast. After the breakfast, all the friends headed for the lake, prepared for prescribed rites and rituals at the banks.

The circumference of the lake is 87 kilometres. The area is about 350 square kilometres. Four rivers originate here. We will talk about that later. We have to circumambulate the lake. But how? It was decided that this would be done on Land Cruisers. 90 kilometres. The depth of this lake at an altitude of 15,000 feet is 300 feet. Tibetans call it Tso Mavang. Oldest lake in human history. When Sage Dattatreya[1] had a vision of Shiva, he asked him, "What is the holiest place on earth?" Shiva replied, "It is in the Himalayas where Kailas and Mansarovar stand." Whoever takes a bath in this lake washes away all his sins. Merely recalling Kailas accrues more merit than a pilgrimage to Kashi. Infinite benefits are gained. Kailas ensures the fulfilment of all four ends of life – *dharma*[2], *artha, kama* and *moksha*[3].

The sky at Mansarovar was such a blue as we had never seen before. White cloud-like flakes of cotton were making patterns. It seemed nymphs were dancing in the horizon. It is claimed in *Shivapurana*[4] that one who bathes in the lake

---

1 *Dattatreya : The great sage considered to be the first guru, yogi and scientist. In many regions of India and Nepal he is worshipped as a deity.*

2 *Dharma : Religion; righteous conduct.*

3 *Moksha : It refers to freedom from samsaara, the cycle of death and rebirth. Moksha refers to emancipation, enlightenment, liberation and release.*

4 *Shivapurana : A major scripture of the Hindu religion extoling the greatness of Lord Shiva.*

ensures the salvation of the next seven generations in his line. I thought this wasn't a chance to be missed; others in the team were a bit hesitant. What if some mishap takes place? Ice-cold water could cause serious illness. And if one fell ill in this remote place, what medical aid could one expect? I said, "Why worry? Don't perform any last rites. Just leave my mortal remains behind. I am content to live here forever. After all, even the Pandavas[1] are here. What can be a better place than this for liberation? This is where ascetics and nymphs, gods and goddesses stay together. This is what we believe as also do the Tibetans." Why delay the dip?

I removed my clothes, draped myself in a *gamchha* (towel). To boost up courage, I remembered the ancestors, bowed to the lake, took a ritual sip of the water – it was sweet as nectar. Felt like an electric shock as I took the first step in water; took another step. Pinched the nostrils and took the dip. Felt I had turned to stone. Limbs were frozen stiff. Things improved a bit with second and third dips. Bones were chattering. The thought crossed my mind that I had come to liberate the forefathers but

---

[1] *Pandava : The five brothers, all sons of King Pandu of Hastinapur kingdom; protagonists of the great war mentioned in the Hindu epic Mahabharata.*

it seemed I myself would join the last of the dear departed.

Just then I sighted a pair of geese, also known as Himalayan Green Finch. Long-necked, majestic, white birds with golden plumes. Only the fortunate see them. By the time I told the friends about them, they had disappeared. Kabir's lines surfaced in the mind: *Ur jayega hansa akela jag darshan ka mela!* (The swan will fly away alone, leaving behind the spectacle of this world!)

Friends were not ready to believe that I had sighted the golden swans. Anyway, I dressed up. Stepped out. Sun-god was nowhere to be seen. After Kailas *darshan* and Mansarovar *snan,* it felt nothing remained to be done. The cold had prompted spontaneous chanting of Mahamrityunjaya *mantra.* I remembered my *Dadi* (grandmother) who was addressed as *Dada* (grandfather) by all of us. It was she who had first told us about Mansarovar and described its sanctity. I offered ritual *arghya*[1] in her memory with consecrated water held in the 'cup' of my joined palms after offering it to Surya. I thought now I had really performed her last rites. Then the thought flashed in my mind, 'Who will

[1] *Arghya : Hindu tradition of offering water to the deities while reciting mantras or prayers.*

come here to do this for me?' The guide, as if reading my mind, said, "Now do the *tarpan* yourself. This is what people do here." I did as advised. Prayed to the water, "Give life, give liberation, ilberate ancestors, wash away all blemishes that mar the mind." As the Hindi poem states, *"Kaat andh ur ke bandhan star, baha janani jyotirmaya nirjhar."*

Tied a prayer flag too on the banks of Mansarovar. Filled up a can with water to take back to Delhi. Then started the *puja*. Kailas in front, Mansarovar on the flank. Had brought *bilvapatra* with me. Anointed Shiva with *bhang*[1] and perfumes – *Trayambakam yajamahe*[2], *sugandhim pushtivardhanam, urvarukaamiva bandhanaam mrityormokshiya maamritaat!* This was a deeply satisfying ritual for us.

---

[1] *Bhang: Crushed leaves of cannabis plant consumed as an intoxicant. It is also offered to Lord Shiva along with thorn apple etc.*

[2] *Triyambakam Yajamahe : One of the most significant Mantras in the Hindu sacred scriptures -Vedas, invoking Lord Shiva.*

I switched on the heater after sitting in the car. Then began to regain my full senses. Now we were circumambulating Mansarovar. Our Land Cruiser seemed to slip and glide slowly on round pebbles on crossing tiny water springs. The water from Mansarovar appeared to flow towards Rakshas Tal at times and in the opposite direction at other. The year when it heads towards Rakshas Tal is considered auspicious for the Tibetans.

Four major rivers in the world flow out from Mansarovar in four different directions. The river in the west is Sutlej. The Tibetans call it Lanjyen Khambab, that translates as elephant's mouth. Karnali flows out to the south. The same river is first called Sarayu and then Ghaghara in India. The Brahmaputra is called Ltamchok Khambab, that means the horse's mouth. It originates on the eastern extremity. The river that is born on the northern side is Sindhu or Sing Chu-lion's mouth. It is also known as Indus.

Our circumambulation is complete as we reach Zaidi.

# Infinity
# ANANT

Tarchen, 40 kilometres away from Zaidi, is the base camp for Kailas *parikrama*. The condition of our friends, particularly the women in the team, dissuaded us from persisting. Skipping Tarchen and returning seemed the best option. En-route we came across a village of shepherds. Our vehicle was driving on a metalled track through a vast plain. The rugged beauty of the plateau was breathtaking. After some time, one could see Tarchen. It was decorated with small prayer flags and buntings. One could also spot a barrack-shaped guesthouse. Tourists can only take vehicles till this point. No vehicle goes beyond. They halt here and there are a few mechanics' workshops and garages along with some Tibetan restaurants. Also a small number of curio shops. Even a small stone picked up here makes a priceless memento and on sale here were regular souvenirs. Our team-mates stopped to splurge on prayer flags, stickers, scarves, kerchiefs and buntings. Lord Shiva and Buddha were in company as their pictures were sold in the same shop.

There are some 300 houses in this settlement. All those who live here are shepherds who herd sheep or goats. Or they subsist on whatever is available, providing services to tourists. There is a school for namesake run by the Red Cross. There

is no hospital or dispensary; patients have to be carried to Takalakot that lies 120 kilometres away. The Red Cross wants to open a hospital here but the Chinese government isn't permitting it. Maybe it is extra cautious because this is a strategically sensitive border area. On each step, you encounter a Chinese soldier. This is the last village with human habitation on the way to Kailas. After this, all you can see is desolate and endless whiteness.

Kailas is seen clearly from Tarchen. 22,000 feet tall Kailas occupies an expanse that is 45 kilometres. It is surrounded by five Buddhist *gomphas. Gomphas* are hut-like monasteries where only a few Buddhist monks perform ritual worship in a token form. Before the Chinese took over Tibet, these *gompha* spirituals enjoyed great power and prestige in the lamaist regime. They had spiritual as well as temporal authority. In 1949, the Buddhist monasteries were razed, burnt and looted. The Chinese revolution turned the *gomphas* into ruins. Later they were repainted and resurrected as shack-like structures, bereft of any trace of their past aura. Many are devoid of doors and windows. For the Buddhists, these are places of worship.

There was a time when the Buddhist *gomphas* were rich repositories of Sanskrit and Pali manuscripts. Many of these were brought back to India, loaded on yaks by the great scholar Mahapandit Rahul Sankrityayan in the 1920s and 1930s. Dalai Lama also carried some volumes with him. But many important manuscripts were burnt by the Chinese. Every *gompha* is scarred by brutal suppression by the Chinese. Terrified monks chant *mantras* in hushed voices. They appear afraid and helpless. Seeing them, one feels both anger and distress at the plight of Tibetans in their homeland.

The Kailas mountain chain stretches up to Bhutan. Kailas stands between Lhatsu and Dzhongchu. The lowest peak is Tarchen and the highest is Desfu Gompha. The circumambulation of Kailas begins at 16,000 feet and climbs up to 19,000 feet.

We proceeded on our way. A wonderful sight greets us. A snow-covered mountain chain between two valleys. Clear blue sky as the backdrop. Specks of white clouds at some places. Waterfalls created by melting snow – seen from a distance, appeared like a stream of milk. I had only seen such streams of milk on Mahashivratri[1] at the Kashi Vishwanath temple.

As we advanced a little, we reached a snow-covered valley. We were told it was here that Mahadev had burned Kamadeva[2]. The place was not snow-clad then. It was a green valley and carpeted with flowers. Spring reigned here throughout the year. The gods were tormented by a demon named Tarak. The went to Brahma to complain. The Creator smiled and told them that Shiva's son would rid them of this menace. Shiva, grief-stricken after the death of Sati, was immersed in deep meditation. How then could he sire a son? Kamadeva was despatched by Indra to wreck his meditation. When Kamadeva reached the spot, the icy wilderness was transformed into a pleasant spring.

Parvati appeared with her companions to worship Shiva. She offered a floral tribute. At this very moment,

---

[1] *Mahashivratri : The great night of Shiva's marriage celebrated by the Hindus every year with great religious fervour and enthusiasm.*

[2] *Kamadev : The Hindu God of love and desire. Son of God Vishnu and Goddess Lakshmi. His wife's name was Rati. Shiva's meditative state was once disrupted by him. It was then that Lord Shiva's rage reached its peak and he opened his third eye to burn down Kamadeva.*

Kamadeva, hidden in nearby bushes, shot a floral arrow and pierced the ascetic's heart. Shiva caught a glimpse of Parvati. Wondered what this beauty was doing here. He was distracted but soon regained his composure and resumed meditation. But couldn't concentrate. After the interruption, Shiva was bewildered. Kamadeva's arrow was doing its work. As Kama smiled, Shiva spotted him. Angry Shiva opened his third eye. Kamadeva was reduced to ashes. Scared, Parvati and her companions made good their escape.

Rati, Kamadeva's wife approached Shiva, crying inconsolably. She beseeched Shiva, "My Lord! What will become of me now?" The kind Lord's heart melted. He spoke out, "I will bring Kamadeva back to life. But from now on, he will exist without a body. He will never appear and will do his work invisibly, targeting his prey stealthily. There will be no everlasting spring – the season that stirs hearts with amorous thoughts – it will last for a couple of months." Ever since, spring visits this land just for two months.

We were now standing by the gate of *Yama*[1] – the only entrance to heaven. The mountain range looked like a gate. Men too had built a gate. Pilgrims pile stones in tiny pyramids. Many such pyramids are seen here. This is the pilgrims' way of

[1] *Yama : The Lord of death in Hindu religion.*

registering their presence. An inscription dating back to the Buddhist period marks a stone near the gate. This was the spot wherefrom Yudhishthir proceeded heavenwards, accompanied only by his dog. Nachiketa's[1] *Yamadwar* is also here. To the right are the *mahasamadhis*[2] of 84 Tibetan *mahasiddhas*[3]. *Mahasamadhi* means the place where the mortal remains of a person are placed for kites and vultures to eat and dispose of. We did not visit the place. Doing so would have meant disrespect to the departed.

This place is also known as *SibaT'sal* or 'death's plateau'. If you reach this spot safely, it is considered to be a rebirth. Murari Bapu[4] is very fond of this place. He has held his *kathashivirs* – story-telling sessions many times. The road beyond Yamadwar is very difficult. Yaks are available to carry the luggage. The source of the Brahmaputra river lies close by.

We were now going to Ashtapada, stumbling and recovering at each step. It is the holiest spot for Jains. Rishabdeva, the first *tirthankara* had forsaken his body after completing the *parikrama* in eight steps. Jains too revere Kailas as much as the Hindus.

---

1 *Nachiketa : The prodigal son of sage Vajashrava, famous for his dialogue with Yama, the Lord of death.*

2 *Samadhi : The highest state of consciousness achieved by a practitioner of yoga.*

3 *Mahasiddhas : In the Vajryaan tradition of Buddhism, the yogis who acquire supernatural powers are called Mahasiddhas.*

4 *Murari Bapu : A religious preacher who gives discourses on the epic 'Ramayana' - the story of Lord Rama.*

Now we are at the southern face of Kailas. You can see Shiva's mount Nandi very close. In fact, this is a bull-shaped rock that is called Mount Nandi. Breathing had become hard. High mountains on all sides, marsh in the middle. I realised the real worth of the Land Cruiser on this rough stretch of undulating track.

Now the steps formed on ice could be clearly seen. It was this staircase that gods had used in the misty past to descend on earth. We were supported by walking sticks. It was impossible to lift the feet to take the next step. On the way, we came across a mongoose-like animal with hare-like movements. Some said it was a mongoose, others called it a squirrel. The guide said, "This is a rodent called Chipi in Tibetan." There were hundreds of Chipis. We drew some satisfaction from the sight. Thank God, at least some form of life thrives at this great height!

Our throats were parched. Lack of oxygen was making us hallucinate a bit. The guide advised us to frequently sip water to avert a headache. Yaks carrying luggage packs were moving along with us. There were a few elderly pilgrims who were performing the *parikrama* on yaks. Some others, infirm and ailing, were carried by Nepalese porters on their back. They too were encountering difficulties. The yak, an independent animal, would break into a canter suddenly or decide to move at a very slow halting pace. Along the narrow mountain path, the yak would move at the very edge of the precipice. The deep valley scared the pilgrims out of their wits. Then the yak would stop for a drink. This four-legged creature is carefree and utterly unpredictable.

Life in Tibet would be impossible without the yaks. They have a special significance on this Roof of the World. If one *parikrama* liberates us, then these yaks have been reformed many times. Just imagine how much good *karma* they must have accumulated! My respect for the creatures suddenly increased manifold. They are noble animals – serious and hard-working. They perform back-breaking work but are never seen aggressive or angry. Tibetans love them dearly. Each yak is lovingly named. But yaks too appear as unfortunate as other beasts of burden – mules and asses. They are never spared torture by the Chinese who kill and eat them.

Our kitchen and rations were being carried on the yak's back. Dinner would be cooked wherever we halted for the night. We used yaks to cross the Brahmaputra. Now our caravan moved towards Derafuk. The road with its steep climb and descent, is extremely tiring. Climbing suddenly and descending sharply. The coolies and guides, everyone was chewing a piece of dried yak meat. We, the Brahmins of Kashi, were left helpless. How then to cope with the cold? There was no vegetarian option so one could do nothing but to shiver in the cold. Further along the *parikrama*, we came across the Lhasa river – the name translates as river of gods – Devnadi. From the banks of the river, one could catch a glimpse of the southern part of Kailas. Lhatsu is called Sindhu river downstream. This stream has to be crossed on a bamboo bridge.

For the first time, on this difficult journey, we felt that we were not heading for Kailas but wandering towards the other world. Hallucinations, nausea and headache – all ailments caused by lack of oxygen. The distressing symptoms were increasing. Exposure to bright snow also caused snow blindness. The eyes seemed to be affected now, although we had worn dark glasses. Snow stretching out in the far distance reminded me of poet Alok: *Paharon ke jism par barf ki chaadar.* Poet's mountains have some limits, but this white sheet appeared without a beginning or end.

The Dolma Pass marks the highest point in the *parikrama* – 19,500 feet, 12,000 feet higher than the Everest base camp. A most difficult and terrifying climb. By the time we reached this spot, we were gasping for breath. The summit of Kailas is just 3,000 feet above Dolma. Felt like reaching out and touching it! Kailas appears most beautiful here like a snow-clad *Shivalinga.* You can palpably feel the stairs to heaven. This is a mountain very different from other peaks – it is a pository of mysterious powers. Perfectly balanced – equal in length and breadth. We stood before it, breathless with great sense of reverence.

From the western extremity of Kailas are seen the wavelets of Sheshnag. The guide told us that these are the marks left behind by the churning of the ocean. Who can be a greater sculpture than Nature? You may recall that when the ocean was churned, it was this mountain that was pressed into service as a giant churner. This huge slab of granite looms large, appearing as a *Shivalinga.* The guide explained it all as he showed us the marks. The route was risky. We had to balance ourselves on large rocks – one false step meant landing straight at the feet of Mahadeva!

Dolma means Taradevi. On top of this pass, she is worshipped. Worship was underway on a rock – lamp, incense, rice grains. Narrow trail, like a fine line, for a footpath. Fellow pilgrims hang prayer flags here. Fifteen minutes is more than enough to endure. There was a severe shortage of oxygen. Tradition enjoins that you leave something behind at Dolma. When the tradition was established, this perhaps referred to some human weaknesses – lies and deceit, ego, addictions, lust and anger – that had to be left behind. Nowadays people leave behind shoes, old clothes, towels and garbage. Those who can't come themselves are represented by their personal effects carried by friends and relatives. All this is symbolic. In the *Gita*, Shri Krishna compared the body to apparels that a soul frequently changes.

We were combating the weather with chants of *Om namah Shivaya!* It was hard to make out in the bitter cold and stifling atmosphere what we were uttering. Only lips moved – we had no control over them. Why do our gods dwell in such difficult places? It seems when gods were sick of crowds, they retired to places where they couldn't be disturbed by hordes of devotees. Despite this, people reach here. Definitely gods are distressed by this. I felt that soon the gods will move out to some other place.

We move towards Lhatsu valley, below Dolma. Now there is a gentle slope. An emerald-coloured freshwater lake – iridescent green – is encountered at the height of 17,000 feet. Oh! This is Gauri Kunda. It has a circumference of seven-and-a-half kilometres and depth of 80 feet. Gauri Kunda remains mostly covered by snow for a major part of the year. One can hear the music of falling water under its cover. Some people removed the snow to take a bath. It is believed that Parvati used to bathe here. Ganesha was born here. Parvati had performed austerities here to win Shiva as her husband.

There is something in the air, water and soil here. I had never felt this with such intensity ever before. A special vibration permeates the atmosphere. The mind is transported to another realm. This is the meditation ground of 84 *mahasiddhas*. One is in the palpable presence of a supernatural power. *Parikrama* continues below Gauri Kunda along the banks of Tsong Chu river. Now Tarchen is only 15 kilometres away. That is where the circumambulation ends. This stretch of the journey was easy.

Just then we saw a unique instance of reverence which can be termed as the height of devotion. Tibetans too have an immense sense of reverence for the Kailas. Some fervent devotees were circumambulating the Kailas. On one hand we were finding it difficult to perform this ritual on foot and they were lying down and crawling to do the same! We bowed to their deep sense of devotion. They were weaving gloves of jute and had tied rubber pads on their knees to traverse the undulated rocky path. In the same manner as we give a contract to Pandits for performing rituals on our behalf, the wealthy perform the ritual of circumambulation through the coolies. God knows who earns the reward of good *Karma* but the coolies appear to be true devotees.

We came back to Tarchen after completing the circumambulation. We were expressing our thanks to each other by reciting *"Om namah Shivaya"* and gradually all of us started regaining strength. I was at a loss to decide who should I thank for this journey.

My being was filled with a feeling of quietude and a deep sense of silence, implicit and beyond expression.

# Lava

# LAVA

Vision of the Lord was enthralling the mind, as the mind is in thrall, so is the body where the mind resides. When the body and mind become one, it is called *chitta*. We started the return journey from Mansarovar. Staring back, turning the neck repeatedly, to catch a glimpse as the vehicle moved on. Kailas was being left behind! Whatever had been gathered was being left behind. Will I ever come here again in this life-time? Lord, only you know this. We are your servants, who do what you will. Do as the master orders.

One thing was hurting repeatedly. Why should our Lord reside in a foreign land? How weak and useless are we that we let go off the place of his residence to a foreign country? I recalled reading Ram Manohar Lohia[1] on the Himalayan policy. His mind was clear. McMahon Line is not the border between India and China. It cannot define the border. He had once asked Nehru, "What kind of people can settle their gods in a foreign country? Maybe smaller deities can be shifted but this can never be allowed to happen to Shiva and Parvati!

[1] *Ram Manohar Lohia : Freedom fighter, socialist leader and politician.*

Had we retained Kailas-Mansarovar, we could have used it to protect Tibet. Tibet, like Nepal, is our brother. And, if Tibet is not independent, we must ensure that the border with China is settled 70-80 miles to the north of the McMahon Line. My answer to those who don't believe that this can be done is that India will not forever be ruled by persons who are impotent."

The anger that moved Dr. Lohia and the pain of subservience is reflected in the eyes of the Tibetans. Whatever silent dialogue happened with them during this journey reflected the helpless anguish and unrest of the people. Chinese oppression forces them to remain silent. They can't open up because the brutal suppression continues. More than 25 Tibetan freedom fighters languish in Chinese jails, preserving embers that await a favourable wind to rekindle the fire. They live in the hope that Tibet will be independent again – tomorrow, if not today! They survive cherishing the dream of an independent Tibet in their hearts. But who will help them regain their independence? India, the elder brother, the mentor and friendly guide has conceded that Tibet is an integral part of China. This has caused a great deal of despair in Tibet.

Before the Chinese arrived in 1950, Tibet had over 6,000 monasteries and shrines where over 6,00,000 monks lived. The Chinese crushed both the Tibetan State and its religion. According to a survey undertaken in 1979, only 60 monasteries survived in Tibet and these too were crumbling and on the verge of extinction. Most of the monks who dwelt here were killed or had gone missing. Monasteries were dynamited so as not to leave behind a trace. Tibet was known as the Roof of the World. It was famous for its herbal forests. The Chinese cut down almost 100 per cent of this precious resource in the name of security considerations.

Tibetan monasteries replicated Indian models. They testified to intimate relations between India and Tibet. We were taught to drink tea by the Tibetans. Chinese have been drinking tea for about, 4,000 years. First they imported tea from China, then started producing and exporting it. Tea reached India via Tibet through mule-track trade.

Before the Chinese invasion, Tibet had never been politically a part of China. The relationship with India can be traced to the advent of Buddhism. The Mongols ruled the land between 1249 and 1368. It was under Manchu domination between 1649 and 1910. After that, it was an independent nation till 1949. It had participated in the Asian Relations Conference convened in Delhi in 1947. Indian currency was in use there and Indians postal services operated.

Contacts between China and Tibet date back to a war in the ninth century. China had to face a disgraceful defeat in this clash of arms in 821. China avenged this defeat in 1951. It occupied Tibet. 80,000 Tibetans lost their lives in this conflict. More than 25,000 Tibetans were put in Chinese jails. They were subjected to inhuman torture. The plan was to settle five million Chinese in Tibet to destroy its civilisation. China exterminated 27 per cent of the total Tibetan population. The Maoist Chinese government called the monks traitors, fifth columnists, vagabonds and thieves in red robes. Dalai Lama escaped that in disguise and came to India, playing hide and seek with Chinese troops hot on his trail. It took him days riding on yak back via Tawang in Arunachal Pradesh. India granted him and his followers political asylum.

This invasion allowed China not only to usurp Tibet's land, but also helped destroy the noble Buddhist creed. It crushed their civilisation. Destroyed the religious books and the libraries were burnt down. This was the bizarre way of the communists to kill the roots of their culture. Forests were cut down where medicinal plants grew. To complete the genocide, Tibet was flooded with people of Han descent. The Hans were atheists and bitter enemies of the Buddhists. Not only the monks were targeted; their beloved yaks too were killed and gobbled up.

The sordid saga of Han oppression continues. The Tibetans are humiliatingly made aware that the Hans are the real owners of Tibet now. Dorji's meek eyes bear testimony to these tortures. One can see how much they have suffered. Perhaps this is why Dr. Lohia had likened the Chinese invasion of Tibet to foeticide.

It is difficult to comprehend what constraints made our government to commit such a blunder in its Tibet policy. This was later called a 'Himalayan blunder'. This can't be undone, however much one wishes. Tibet stood like a strong wall – natural barrier between India and China. A buffer zone. China now breathes down our neck after Tibet has ceased to exist. Its border touches Indian territory, from Chamoli in Uttarakhand to Tawang in Arunachal Pradesh. We are facing incursions and intrusions by the Chinese. In 2011 itself, the Chinese violated the Indian border 108 times. In 2012, the number increased to over 500.

We are reaping what we have sown. Why did we make this mistake? No one has any answer. When Nehru had called Tibet an independent nation in 1935, why did he change his mind after the Chinese attack? After the hostilities, he merely echoed what Mao claimed. Both agreed that Tibet was an internal matter of China. We were busy chanting Hindi-Chini *Bhai-Bhai*[1], while China was preparing to attack us treacherously.

The attack came. We lost. The Chinese also impacted Mansarovar pilgrimage. We were deprived of our Kailas. When the Janata government came to power, the then Foreign Minister, Atal Bihari Vajpayee, held many rounds of talks with China to reopen the pilgrim route. The government fell but the efforts continued. Subramanian Swamy[2] persisted. His ceaseless striving bore fruit and the government of Deng Sia Ping issued special permits for pilgrimage. The first band of pilgrims led by Subramanian Swamy to Mansarovar included Harish Rawat. Since then, the pilgrimage continues on the basis of stapled visas.

Tibetans feel a natural affinity towards visitors from India. They have hopes. We were trying to find out some details about Chinese oppression from Dorji, our driver. He was sharing his experiences in discrete bits. He found out during this conversation that I belonged to Benaras.

Suddenly his conduct changed. He started kissing my hands. Tears streamed from his eyes. As evening descended, he took me to a secluded spot and asked questions about Sarnath and Rimpoche. Then I disclosed that I have also met the Dalai Lama. He was wonderstruck and kept staring at me. He suddenly prostrated himself in front of me. I was stunned. This generation of Tibetans hasn't seen Dalai Lama. The have only read and heard about him. Dalai Lama is a legend and lore for them. He is God for them. Maybe he saw an angel in me.

Chinese soldiers stood only a short distance away. To talk about the Dalai Lama or to keep his photographs is considered sedition there; a punishable offence. I was scared. I had landed myself in strange trouble. I lifted him and embraced

---

[1] *Hindi-Chini Bhai-Bhai : Literally, Indians and Chinese are brothers – a slogan given by Prime Minister Jawaharlal Nehru after the accord signed with Chinese Premier, Zhou En-lai in 1954.*

[2] *Subramanian Swamy : Professor, economist and politician of India who relentlessly lobbied with the Chinese government for the opening of the Kailas Mansarovar route for pilgrims.*

him. Explained everything, ensuring that the Chinese soldiers shouldn't get suspicious or get a clue of what we were talking about. I told Dorji that Rimpoche is a family friend. He visits our home and I have known him since my childhood. He was a member of my marriage party; adding that I had sought his blessings before embarking on this journey and would see him on return.

Dorji became emotional. He left me standing and disappeared. I was keeping an eye on the Chinese soldiers standing by the vehicle. Suddenly some 20-25 lamas materialised as if from nowhere in that desolate spot. One kept on kissing my hand while the other did the same with the forehead. Yet another was touching his rosary beads to my body. They were deeply moved but for me, it was a embarrassing moment.

I had come here to have a vision of God but here I had become an object of adoration and reverence! I was getting restless witnessing their faith. I considered making good my escape before the lamas did something unpredictable in their fervour for Dalai Lama and Rimpoche and the Chinese suspected me of being an intruding spy. Taking long steps, I returned to the resthouse, but their faith kept steering my being along the way.

The present Dalai Lama, Tenzin Gyatso, is 14th in the lineage. In the Tibetan system, the Dalai Lama is the head of the State as well as the supreme spiritual preceptor. This was the system that prevailed in Tibet before the Chinese invasion. Dalai Lama is a Mongolian title that translates as 'ocean of knowledge'. In Tibet, he is believed to be an incarnation of the Buddha. The present Dalai Lama is considered to be 74th among such incarnation. He is the real voice of the Tibetan people. He is worshipped by Tibetans all over the world. No one else living on this planet is showered with such adulation. His status is much higher than that of a supreme religious leader. People are ready to die for him.

Tibetans belong to the Mahayana[1] sect of Buddhism and represent a society naturally inclined towards a nomadic way of life. It has evolved with passage of time as a society where ownership of the land belongs to the State but as a property, it remains in the joint control of the government, monasteries and the elite.

The mind raced against intelligence. Land divided by borders was being left behind. We couldn't call the land of our gods our own. Had come here as pilgrims; were returning now as foreigners. We were returning from Mansarovar; our Kailas was being separated from us.

---

[1] *Mahayana : Literally – the great vehicle; one of the three main branches of Buddhism; 'Thervada' and 'Vajrayana' being the other two.*

## Separation

# PARTHKYA

A range of mountains one after the other in an endless series. We were on our way back, crossing these mountains continuously. Clear blue sky above and down below an infinite expanse of white. The road was curvaceous, but broad and smooth. I carried a can full of water from Mansarovar and some pebbles for the sake of remembrance. The physical body was returning home but the heart was at Kailas Mansarovar.

We had managed to reach here due to extra-ordinary support and luck. But, oh Lord! How can your real devotees – the retinue of the poor, underprivileged, exploited, downtrodden, oppressed and the wretched manage to come here? They have nothing to offer you but a *lota* full of water. Please make this pilgrimage easier for them.

Those who are unable to reach Kailas have found Kailas within their reach. Himachal Pradesh has Kinnar Kailas and Uttarakhand is home to Chhota Kailas.

Perhaps the best example of re-construction of Kailas symbolically is the Kailasnath temple at Ellora[1]. This was built by the rulers of the Rashtrakuta[2] dynasty, who carved it out of a giant rock. It seems that to reside in the south, Shiva himself took the form of a mountain. The sculptures carved on the walls depict the story of Ravana's penance on it, along with enchanting scenes of Shiva's celestial love-play with Parvati.

So much about the desire to locate Kailas within our own comfort zone. But those who wish to visit

---

[1] *Ellora : Rock-cut caves and temples of Hindu, Buddhist and Jain religious faith. Built near Auragabad district of Maharashtra between 200 BC to AD 1000 world heritage site.*

[2] *Rashtrakuta : A royal dynasty in a large part of the Indian sub-continent between the 6th and 10th centuries.*

Mansarovar in a group, organised by the government, have to overcome many obstacles. First the External Ministry invites applications through an advertisement printed in newspapers. Then a lottery is drawn because the government can send only 500 persons in a year. The government gives a subsidy to these pilgrims. Each has to submit an affidavit before a magistrate, testifying that if his soul departs, no one should be held responsible for the body en route and the family will not sue for claims! Then you have to clear a tough medical test to secure a certificate that you are fit to trek above the altitude of 19,000 feet. After all, the vagaries of weather will decide your fate.

The lottery to begin with, then health, followed by weather – you can't help anything, but pray to Baba Bholenath. You may opt for the route through Uttaranchal, journeying on foot or take off in a helicopter or motor vehicle via Nepal. But all have to tread on foot after Tarchen. No elephants, horses to ride nor carts to transport you in comfort when you go to meet your Maker.

On the return journey, we could see just before Takalakot, on the desert-like plateau, Buddhist monasteries, hundreds of years old. Very few visit them. As a matter of fact, these structures should be called ruins of monasteries rather than monasteries. Two portraits are displayed in every monastery. Guru Padmasambhava, the legendary sage adept at *tantra* and credited with bringing Buddhism to Tibet in the 8th century, seated in the classic posture of a seeker. The other is Milarepa, the greatest of Tibet's poet-saints. He lived in the 11th century and was believed to enjoy supernatural powers. Tibetans sing his songs to this day. Ties between Milarepa and Nathpanthi[1] sect of India can also be traced. The lineage of gurus leads us to Guru Gorakhnath and his preceptor, Guru Matsyendranath.

[1] *Nathpanth : A religious sect born out of the mingling of two major sects of the Hindu religion—'Shaiva' and 'Shakti'*

Milarepa was a protégé mentored by Tilopa, who in turn had been enlightened by Kankanappa. He, in turn, was tutored by Adinath who is believed to be Shiva incarnate. The lineage of the gurus of Gorakhnath also takes us to Adinath in Tibet. Gorakhnath and Matsyendranath are revered not only in Tibet, but also in Nepal. The Gorkha community derives its name from Gorakhnath; Gorkha is also the name of a province. People of Tibet eulogise Milarepa for his close relations with Indian *tantrics*. Tibet presents a unique confluence of Shaiva and Buddhist *tantric* practices rarely witnessed in South-east Asia.

We had just reached Takalakot when our driver informed us that the cenotaph of Zoravar Singh is close by. Odd, but interesting. Our driver had turned into a mythic at narrator, *Kakbhusundi*. He told us the story of Zoravar Singh. Zoravar Singh was a General commanding Maharaja Gulab Singh's army. He had the ambition to annex Ladakh and Baltistan into his Hindu kingdom and so include Kailas in his domain. He had succeeded when, trapped in a snow blizzard, his troops surrendered. Zoravar Singh was killed. His memorial stands 5 kilometres away from Takalakot. It's just a mound of clay. The Chinese don't usually allow the

pilgrims to go there. Dorji showed us a photograph of the tomb and told us that the villagers worship there. They believe that the spirit lying here can repel evil spirits. It was getting late, so we decided against going there despite a strong desire to do so. As we descended, losing height, our spirits revived. We only halted at Takalakot because the kitchen van had camped there and cooked dinner. We also had to return the wind-cheaters and jackets to the guide who had lent these to use as protection against snow and ice. We had to acknowledge our debt for such a divine trip made enjoyable by his aid and advice. He had to return to Kathmandu at once, with his three associates.

In the same truck, it would have taken them two days to return. We ate *khichdi* hurriedly, removed his heavy gear and dressed in our own woollens. Bid farewell. Sherpas had been with us for just two days but separation was not without painful pangs. He was the guide, cook and doctor. I bent down to touch his feet.

We headed for Hilsa. Dorji was sad. He knew that we will part in a few moments. His company made us feel as if we had known each other for ages. The vehicle stopped at the border-post. Chinese police was conducting immigration and custom checks. Cameras were carefully inspected to ensure that no pictures of sensitive areas were taken. When free from the border-post, Dorji got down from the vehicle. He offered to walk along with us across the bridge, carrying our luggage, I tried to dissuade him, but to no avail. His affection made it impossible to part ways.

I agreed on the condition that he would come only till a part of the Laxman Jhula-like hanging bridge that lies in Tibet. I turned back to cast a last look at Tibet and felt that strong sense of attachment. It felt as if I was walking away, leaving behind my own street in Benaras. As we reached the bridge, I gifted Dorji my jacket that was bought specially for the trip to Tibet. He was overjoyed like a child as we crossed the bridge. Dorji kept shouting, *'Bum Bhole. Om namah Shivaya!'* We could hear him till we lost sight of him. That voice continues to echo in my ears even today. We could see our helicopter across the river. Our luggage was loaded in the helicopter. Due to the high altitude, we were to be transported in two batches. As the chopper couldn't fly over the sky-scraping peaks, we landed in Simikot. A small plane to take us to Nepalganj was ready to take off. But the chopper had to return to fetch our friends. Everyone's luggage was loaded on the plane. This exercise was done in order to lighten the load on the chopper. Now we all had to embark for Nepalganj, in the helicopter.

Suddenly, a crisis cropped up without warning. We were asked to disembark from the helicopter that had been revved up. I couldn't understand what was happening. We looked at each other anxiously. Something was seriously amiss. "We are checking up the helicopter," said the captain. Everyone was waiting, wondering what was happening. It took an hour to refuel the helicopter,

after siphoning out fuel once, to check for any obstruction. By now I could comprehend what was wrong. The fuel gauge in the chopper wasn't working. I had acquired a private pilot's licence in 1979 and had about 110 hours' experience of flying small planes. The captain told me there wasn't anything wrong seriously but an alarm bell was ringing because of this glitch. The fault couldn't be set right even after an hour of tinkering by several people.

After some time, the captain came with the offer to ferry us in two batches. We weren't sure that the flight would not encounter any trouble on the way. We suggested that he call for another helicopter in case of the slightest doubt. We were prepared to wait here till then. But he was ready to take off.

Four of us took off in the first batch. Within minutes, we were above dangerously high peaks. The alarm rang again. I could read lines of worry on the face of our pilot. He was talking to the Air Traffic Control. He was advised to force land at once. I was sitting in front, while the other friends were seated at the back. But all of us could sense that something was wrong. A small village could be sighted below. It appeared from the fuel drums stacked there that at times some planes landed there. After dropping us, avoiding any risk, the helicopter took off for Simikot with the hope that it may return after the fault was set right.

This location was godforsaken with no arrangements for stay. Our phones were not working here. There were no shops selling eatables. Just then a soldier of the Nepal Army arrived. We inquired about the distance to Nepalganj, our destination. "Mules will take five days to cover the bridle path; then two more days by bus," he answered. I asked, "What if we turn back to Simikot where at least boarding and lodging

are available and that's where our friends are stranded?" He said, "Four days on mule track." We were now engulfed in deep despair. Our hearts in our mouths.

In distress, we remembered Lord Bholenath. Surely we made some mistake, committed some lapse. It was a tough test. Waiting wasn't easy. Suddenly a brainwave struck. I asked the soldier if he had any means to communicate with his officers. Could he check if they had any information about us?

Evening was setting in fast. Soon it would become too dark for any helicopter to land or take off. Cold would be unbearable and we did not have enough warm clothes to cope with it. By now some vagrant youth, appearing to be high, had assembled, amused at the sight of stranded strangers. Things were getting a bit scary. It was a great relief to see the soldier running back to us. He revived us with the good news that the ATC has information about the forced landing and that a rescue helicopter is on its way.

Eyes remained fixed on the sky. Where is the helicopter? Why hasn't it reached? Then we could spot a helicopter. We rushed towards it as soon as it landed. The pilot appeared like an angel and soon we were airborne. This time the pilot was flying very low. We were already scared. God forbid, we shouldn't hit a hill. After a tense flight of an hour-and-a-half, we made a happy landing at Nepalganj. The rest of our party had to spend the night at Simikot since the sun had set by then. Helicopter couldn't reach there. We were told that they would join us the next morning. And so they did.

Our dream was realised. Whatever we saw and experienced was beyond comprehension. Its beyond me to describe the amazement at this sacred wonderland. My wayward heart is reluctant to admit that the journey was over. It remained stuck there. I thank you my Lord again and again for calling us from afar, inspiring us and giving us strength. I am grateful to these eyes who allowed us to see all that we saw. And acknowledge my debt to the body that supported us; the mind that received myriad stimuli. Now for you, dear readers, comes this offering from the same heart that has lived these experiences.

# The Routes
# AYAN

## How to reach Kailas and Mansarovar

This is arguably the most difficult and most beautiful journey in the world. This millennia-old pilgrimage has many wonderful ways in which it can be accomplished. The distance between Delhi and Kailas-Mansarovar is approximately 900 kilometres. It takes one to heights from 15,000 to 19,000 feet, whichever route one chooses. There is no insurance available. Embarking on this journey requires strong resolve and psychological strength, no less than exceptional physical stamina.

There are three ways to reach Kailas. One passes through Uttarakhand in India. This is tough and a large part includes trekking on foot. The Government of India sends people along this route. The second route is a little easier. The distance between Kathmandu and Kailas is covered by motor road. The Nepal government opens this route for pilgrims only between June and September. There is a third route also – the easiest, but also the most expensive. This is by

air – taking a helicopter from Nepalganj to Simikot and Hilsa, and then boarding Land Cruisers for Takalakot and beyond.

Kailas-Mansarovar *Yatra* is organised by the Ministry of External Affairs every year. The government sends 16 batches of 60 pilgrims each between May 29 and September 26. The duration of the trip is 28 days. Every pilgrim is allowed to carry 25 kg of luggage, out of which, 5 kg can be of foodstuff. The Indian aspirants for this pilgrimage must be between 18 and 70 years of age. Keeping the rigours of the journey, only those physically fit and in good health are permitted. They alone have to bear the costs and undertake full responsibility for the risks and unforeseen consequences.

## First Option

Kailas-Mansarovar from India

Haldwani-Kausani-Bageshwar-Dharchula-Tawaghat-Pangu-Sirkah-Malpa-Budhi-Gunji-Kalapani-Lipu Lekh Pass-Takalakot-Zaidi-Barkha Maidan-Tarchen-Derafuk-Shri Kailas

## Journey Both Ways

- **On the Indian side:** 14 days (27 kilometres on foot, 1,306 kilometres by bus, i.e. total 1,433 kilometres).
- **On the Chinese side:** 13 days (53 kilometres on foot, 411 kilometres on bus, total 464 kilometres), i.e. entire trip: 27 days (180 kilometres on foot, i.e. total 1,717 kilometres).

This route that passes through Askot, Khel, Grabiang, Lipulekh, Khind in Uttarakhand to reach Takalakot is comparatively difficult. It is 338 miles longer and has many ups and downs along the way. There are many *dharmashalas* and *ashramas* on this route and one can hire porters and yaks for the road ahead at Garbyang. Takalakot is the first halt on the Tibetan side on this route. The journey from Delhi to Kathgodam is undertaken by train and from Kathgodam to Dharchula it is via bus. Then the foot-march begins. Traversing mountain paths for 75 kms, after Gunji, the pilgrims cross over to Tibet at Lipu Lekh Pass (16,500 feet), where the Government of India hands over the travellers to the Chinese authorities. Pilgrims have followed this traditional route for millennia. It was blocked after the Sino-Indian border dispute and the clash of armies in 1962. The *yatra* was resumed only in 1981 due to the efforts of Shri Atal Bihari Vajpayee and Subramanian Swamy.

# Second Option

## Kailas-Mansarovar via Nepal

This route was opened by Nepal a few years back. Private Nepalese travel agencies authorised by the Chinese conduct tours on this route. The round trip takes 15 days. All permits and other formalities are completed in Delhi. Then after a strict medical check-up, you are transported straight to Kathmandu. You may take a stop-over here and visit the Pashupatinath shrine. This is what most people do. Onward journey is on Land Cruisers.

An hour away from Kathmandu, the travel documents are examined by the Chinese officials at the Friendship Bridge, that marks the Nepal-China border. After the checking, one proceeds to the first stage at Nablam. Nablam is in Tibet and is at an altitude of 3,700 metres. This night halt is necessary for acclimatisation. The vehicles target to cover a distance of 260-270 kilometres a day. By evening, the caravan reaches Saga. Next day you embark for Prayang, some 270

kilometres away. This is where you stay at night after 10 hours on the road. Beautiful natural scenery and devotion to Shiva do not allow you to feel tired. Everyone is excited about 'seeing' Mansarovar the next day. Just five days after departure from Delhi, you are in the divine presence of this lake. From this side, you can see the southern part of Mount Kailas also. To perform the *parikrama* of Kailas, you have to reach Tarchen base camp, that is 60 kilometres away from the Mansarovar Lake. The *parikrama* has to be performed on foot or riding a pony. It is not easy to negotiate the circumambulation circuit that covers 54 kilometres.

On the fifth day of the journey, you touch 18,800 feet. The road is like steps – climbing up and down and, at times, plain. There is lack of oxygen due to the height. As soon as you start on foot towards Derafuk, a number of springs and waterfalls are encountered. A refreshing cool breeze revitalises you. You will see Gauri Kunda on the same day when 24 kilometres are covered. During the *parikrama*, you can see the western, northern and southern faces.

## Third Option

### By air from Nepal to Kailas-Mansarovar

The third option to reach Kailas-Mansarovar from India is by air. Helicopter to Kailas is the easiest way.

Kathmandu to Nepalganj and then on to Simikot and Hilsa. There Land Cruisers are available at Hilsa to take you to Mansarovar. One can alternatively travel to Lhasa by China Air and wherefrom you can head for Mansarovar, passing through Tibetan towns of Shingate, Gyantse, Lhatse and Prayang.

Kathmandu to Nepalganj is a one-hour flight. Then one takes off for Simikot. One must halt here for the night. To acclimatise as also to complete immigration and custom formalities. This is the last administrative outpost on the Nepalese border. One must show all the travel documents here. After completing all the formalities, you wing off for Hilsa. After landing at Hilsa, River Karnali is crossed on a hanging bridge. The travel documents are examined again; this time by the Chinese officials. After this, it takes about an hour by road to reach Takalakot. This takes very little time.

- **Nepalganj to Simikot by helicopter**
  An hour-and-half

- **Simikot to Hilsa by helicopter**
  30 minutes

- **Hilsa to Shergaon on foot**
  One hour

- **Shergaon to Takalakot by Land Cruisor**
  One hour

You must halt at Takalakot to acclimatise. You may visit the old temple at Khojarnath dedicated to Sri Rama, Lakshman and Sita. An 1,100-year-old monastery is also worth visiting. On a Land Cruiser, it takes 45 minutes to reach there. Next morning, the drive to Mansarovar takes an-hour-and-a-half. You pass Rakshas Tal on the way and can indulge in photography to your heart's content for its breathtaking natural scenery.

From Takalakot to Mansarovar is 72 kilometres. After ritual bathing and worship there, one heads for Tarchen, the base camp for Mount Kailas. Tarchen is 40 kilometres from Lake Mansarovar. Tarchen to Yamdwara is 45 minutes. This takes an hour. Beyond Yamdwara, one must walk for the remaining part of this journey. The way back from Derafuk to Dolma Pass is on foot again. Return to Tarchen via Gauri Kunda, then to Takalakot. Cross the border at Hilsa to board the helicopter for return journey to Nepalganj.

**Please note:**

- Respect the mountains. Do not try to conquer them. Don't try to show off your physical prowess. Walk in a column, following a set rhythm. Ensure that you are never without a companion. There is no insurance against sudden illness or any unfortunate accident.
- Lightning strikes are common here. In case of thunder and lightning, avoid contact with wireless equipment and ice axe. Stay away from trees, pointed rocks. Don't take shelter under a tall tree. It is safer to remain in open.
- Do not wear a couple of tight woollens. Instead, use many loose-fitting garments to keep chilly winds out.
- Carry at least two pairs of good-quality trekking shoes with you. Get used to walking with these shoes to avoid discomfort during the pilgrimage.
- Wear at least a pair, each of cotton and woollen socks.
- Ensure that your feet are dry. Use talcum powder before wearing socks. Change the socks as soon as you reach the camp. Wet socks cause discomfort and blisters can trigger skin ailments.
- Use tight-fitting gloves to protect your fingers. The extremities of hands and feet as well as the face need adequate protection from cold. Their constant exposure to cold can reduce body temperature to dangerous levels.
- Drink a lot of fluid while climbing. Hot sweet beverages are best to provide energy at high altitude.
- Use good-quality sunglasses.
- Don't neglect small cuts, bruises and minor injuries. Treat those at once.
- Keep your limbs in motion. Do small exercises at frequent intervals. This is necessary to keep the body warm.
- Don't lose track of the companions. If caught in heavy snowfall or a blizzard, stay closely huddled. Travel in small batches.
- Begin early to reach your destination well in time.
- Don't walk alone or as a couple, don't get separated from the main group of climbers. Keep an eye on the person walking in front.
- Don't sleep with your shoes on.
- Weakness and uneasiness are common during hard treks. You must ensure a supply of glucose and Electral.
- If struck by hunger pangs, opt for small snacks, biscuits and dried fruits and nuts instead of a heavy meal so that you can continue without any discomfort.
- Women should dress in a manner that is comfortable for riding and walking.
- The weather is very unpredictable during the circumambulation. Rains make it harder to walk. Keep waterproof shoes, bands and a light raincoat for protection.
- Torches, candles, matchboxes, needles and thread will save you a lot of bother.
- Keep handy the essential telephone numbers for assistance booths along the way.
- It can be hazardous to bathe at Mansarovar for long and beyond your body's endurance.
- Even if you think you don't require these, make arrangements for porters and ponies. You never know when these may be needed. They are useful both as guide and companion.
- When clicking pictures, take care to exclude both Indian and Chinese military camps.
- This area is largely snow-clad. Use Vaseline or any skin-care lotion liberally on your face and hands to avoid chaffing and cuts and bruises.

| S.NO. | NAME | SIGN |
|---|---|---|
| 1. | METALLED ROAD | |
| 2. | FOOT TRACK | |
| 3. | IMP. PLACES | |
| 4. | N/HALT | |
| 5. | RIVER | |
| 6. | WAY TO KAILASH | |
| 7. | RETURN WAY TO DELHI | |